Pulling Back the Covers

the Covers

5 KEYS TO HELP WOMEN
BREAK FREE FROM PORN &
MASTURBATION ADDICTION

Tenita C. Johnson

Published by So It Is Written, LLC
Detroit, MI
SoItIsWritten.net

Pulling Back the Covers: 5 Keys to Help Women Break Free from Porn &
Masturbation Addiction
Copyright © 2024 by Tenita C. Johnson

Edited by: So It Is Written – www.SoItIsWritten.net

Formatting: Ya Ya Ya Creative – YaYaYaCreative@gmail.com

ISBN: 979-8-9888204-3-7

LCCN: 2024903237

PRINTED AND BOUND IN THE UNITED STATES OF AMERICA

TABLE OF CONTENTS

INTRODUCTION

John 14:21 (MSG) says, *The person who knows my commandments and keeps them, that's who loves me. And the person who loves me will be loved by my Father, and I will love him and make myself plain to him.*

As I sat on the side of the bed for what felt like the thousandth time after doing *that*, I clearly heard God say, "*When you love me enough, you'll keep my commandments. You won't follow any other voice but mine.*"

Now, in my religious mindset and limited head space, I replied, "*God, of course I love you!*"

But in that moment, which immediately followed maybe five short minutes of masturbation and indulging in porn, it was crystal clear that God wasn't sure I loved Him. After all, His Word is clear in John 14:21. It's one thing to know His commandments; it's another to *keep* them. And I'm not talking about those times when I followed His commandments once or twice. He was looking for a lifestyle. His Word didn't say those who *tried* His commandments and decided they just couldn't do it. His Word didn't say those who tried to keep His commandments but fell off after the first week. He was requiring me to be all in or all the way out.

Even though I'd been on several praise teams and several prayer teams, hosted several small groups, sang in numerous choirs and volunteered at many youth retreats, I was failing at *keeping* His commandments. I knew *of* His commandments. I'd heard the Scriptures repeatedly. I'd prayed and fasted when prompted by my spiritual leaders and pastors. But one thing I've come to learn about the Word of God is that, when God uses the word *know*, He means intimately. He's not talking about head knowledge; He's talking about heart knowledge. And while I had mastered all of the religious rhetoric, spiritual exercises and masks in order to push through in ministry, the truth was my heart was far from Him.

It took me years to learn, but I realized the thoughts to masturbate or watch porn intensified when I was alone. My elementary school teacher, Mrs. Cooper, used to say, "An idle mind is the devil's workshop." Even if I had twenty minutes free in my day, during those twenty minutes, here came the thoughts. The darts. The arrows. And, honestly, all it takes is one thought. If I pondered on it long enough, I acted on it. Sure, I regretted it later. I was tired, almost exhausted, after every time. It would drain me every time. I was relieved in my flesh, but I was exhausted in my spirit. Normally, after a quick peep show of porn and/or masturbation, I immediately went to sleep. I had to take a nap. I slept hard, often having crazy dreams that made absolutely no sense in the natural. Although my mind wasn't always idle for a long time, when it was, Mrs. Cooper's warning manifested right away.

Let's be clear. I didn't have to be stimulated or see anything for the thought to enter my mind. If I simply sat still for a few minutes, if I sat in silence for just sixty seconds, the thought would come. It was always there, ready to take advantage of every opportunity and suck the life and energy out of me for the day. What I didn't realize at the time was that God was always there. He was right there.

> *However, this was explicitly written to unlock and unchain Christian women, and women of other various faiths, who claim to love God and follow Him, yet find themselves touching themselves more than they've ever touched the heart and hand of God.*

Even though I had to close the blinds, pull the shades, get under the cover, and turn all the lights out, He was still right there. I'm not sure if it was the shame and guilt, or if I truly believed that God "couldn't see me" because I was under the covers and the lights were off. The room had to be dark. I could never masturbate or watch porn with the lights on.

It took me years to unpack the wounds, the scars and the trauma that had set me on the trajectory that would not only change my level of intimacy with my husband, but my intimacy with God. Even in a pitch-black room, if you shine a flashlight or a spotlight in the room, it will light up whatever area it is shined upon. And I had to learn the hard way that the quickest way to rid my world, and the world at-large, of darkness, is to shine a light in the midst of darkness.

This book isn't about church; it's about *being* the church. It's not about condemnation; it's about walking in truth and freedom in your relationship with the Father. It's not about exposing my business because, at the end of the day, it's all God's business. I would much rather stand boldly in my truth and freedom of what God has delivered me from than mask my hidden, secret sins, only to be later exposed as I am elevated in the Kingdom of God. More importantly, this book isn't just about my freedom. It's about *yours*.

If you've read this far, by now, you know this book is for you. This isn't the book for the person who watches porn or masturbates once every six months—even though there is much to glean for a person in that situation. However, this was explicitly written to unlock and unchain Christian women, and women of other various faiths, who claim to love God and follow Him, yet find themselves touching themselves more than they've ever touched the heart and hand of God. This book is for the bruised and the broken who *want* to be healed and made whole. I realize that not all women in society see an issue with pornography or masturbation. But I'm talking to the woman who wants to be 120% sold out for Jesus and keep His commandments, no matter what dart the enemy throws their way.

So, buckle your spiritual seat belt and prepare to be challenged, transformed and delivered. The enemy told me I'd never be free from my loyalty to porn and masturbation. He told me it was simply my thorn in my side. After all, everyone has their *thing*. You know, that one thing that every Christian who's trying to walk the straight and narrow can't seem to shake. For some, it's alcohol. For others, it's cigarettes. For many, it's food, but I don't have the time or the patience to tackle that generational sin in this book. I promised the Lord if He ever allowed me to be free, and absolutely truly free, I would go back and pull others up and out.

It's time to remove the masks. It's time to pull back the covers. It's time to peel back the layers so you stand blameless and shameless before God. You always have a choice, and personal healing is always your responsibility. If you're ready to break free for good and live the abundant life God intended for you before the foundation of the world was set, turn the page at your own risk!

UNDER THE COVERS

"*If* you have to do it in the dark … if you have to do it under the covers … if you have to do it when no one is home … *it's sin*."

That's what I heard the Lord say to me after I cleaned myself up for what I *wanted* to be the last time.

For years, I battled with whether or not watching porn and masturbating was even a sin. After all, I knew Christian married couples who agreed to watch porn together in order to "enhance" their marriage. That's what I convinced myself of in order to keep repeating the same cycle daily and, sometimes, hourly. I needed it almost as a tutorial on how to best please my husband in the bedroom. After all, someone taught me to ride a bike. But no one taught me how to ride a man. Someone taught me to roller skate. But no one had taught me how to "successfully have sex" and please my husband. Everyone was doing it. Saved and unsaved friends and family alike told me that watching porn and masturbating was okay. I even had a counselor tell me it was "normal" for women to pleasure themselves. That's when I knew it was time for me to find a new counselor.

When I was single, in my mind, I reasoned with God that watching porn and masturbating was much better than having sex with another man. It wasn't fornication, and it wasn't adultery because I wasn't married. I didn't see specific Scriptures about masturbation, so I thought it was a free-will type of thing. When I got married, I thought that would douse the fire of lust. But that lust craved to be quenched daily. However, my appetite increased all the more. Even after intimacy with my husband, two days later, that appetite screamed louder than the moment before. It was never satisfied.

Unfortunately, over the years, I'd programmed myself to be stimulated quickly, multiple times a day. That, in turn, left me always searching for the next high, the next hit, the next level of climax. I realized I had committed adultery on my husband long before I had the extramarital affair after we'd been married ten years. If you missed that story or you're new to my readership, read about that in our marriage anthology, *Marriage Uncut: Straight Talk, No Chaser.*

In 1 Corinthians 7:4, the Word tells us, *The wife does not have authority over her own body but yields it to her husband. In the same way, the husband does not have authority over his own body but yields it to his wife.* According to this Scripture,

I no longer had authority over my own body once I married. So, in essence, I may as well have been having sex with someone else's spouse!

As if that wasn't a big enough wake-up call for me, a pastor friend of mine told me that porn and masturbation were a form of prostitution. I was offended! I was appalled! *Was this joker calling me a prostitute?* I'd been many things in my lifetime. I'd even been called many things by many people. One thing I never considered myself to be, though, was a prostitute. I'd read about Rahab in the Bible. I knew the "after-hours" joints existed, but I'd never set foot in one. To make matters worse, my pastor friend told me I

> *Even with Satan's suggestions, we have a choice. We have free will.*

was a prostitute who was working for *free*. After all, it didn't cost me money to touch myself. Most of the porn I watched was on a DVD or free pay-per-view channels we had for the weekend through our cable provider. I never paid for porn. But whenever I had access to it at no cost, it was absolutely always my pastime of choice.

I thought that, because I didn't pay for it, it wasn't *that bad*. I thought I could stop at any time and that I could control it, but I was only *partially* free. As a teenager, after school, when no one else was home yet, I watched porn or masturbated daily. Eventually, I graduated to the point where I may have only masturbated three times a week and watched porn twice a week. It truly depended on how busy I was (or was not). That was a big part of my problem. When I had hours of free time on my hands, masturbation or watching porn and then taking a nap was always the immediate suggestion from the inner me.

So many people blame the enemy, Satan, for their problems. What I soon found out is that Satan only has to plant a seed, a thought, an idea, once for us to meditate on that thought before we act on it. Even with Satan's suggestions, we have a choice. We have free will. Everyone is a slave to something or someone. I realized that anything, or anyone, I listened to more than I did, the voice of God became my god! Porn and masturbation were my idols. So many times, we think an idol has to be a statue or figure that we worship or put our hope into. Some people depend on sage and incense. Some people depend on drugs or alcohol. Again, some people look to food to be their comforter when God never intended for His people to be comforted by anyone or anything but Holy Spirit. For me, that god, that idol, was addiction to porn and masturbation—even in my marriage.

My addiction to porn and masturbation definitely set me up for failure in marriage. Not only did I expect my husband to perform like the men performed in pornographic videos, but I tried to duplicate some of the positions and soon found out that I was out of shape. I wasn't as flexible as I was in high school during track and cross country. I also discovered my husband is not a robot. Most women assume that men can and will have sex at-will any time, any day, anywhere! That is the furthest thing from the truth.

In addition, because I'd been molested by both men and women, getting comfortable enough to relax and enjoy sex was a mental challenge for me. Almost every time, my husband had to tear down the imaginary walls I'd set up over time to protect myself. Even though we'd been together off and on for more than ten years before we married, something had shifted. In addition to my legs locking up and stiffening during intercourse, new triggers arose. He couldn't hit me on the butt. He couldn't kiss me a certain way. With all of my rules, regulations and restrictions, he stopped initiating sex for a season because he felt like I was rejecting him. In a sense, I was overstimulated in some areas and under stimulated in others.

I thought when I got married that I'd be cured of my addiction. After masturbating and watching porn at least every other day—sometimes, every day—only a bullet vibrator could get me to climax in under five minutes and put me to sleep like a baby. There was only one problem: I was married, and I had made the porn, the masturbation, the rabbit and the bullet replacements for my husband whenever he wasn't available. But even when he was available, more times than not, I had already pleased myself once or twice for the day, so I wasn't interested. He didn't have a fair shot— and it had absolutely nothing to do with him.

Through the triggers and the trauma, I learned how, when and where to stimulate myself to get to the point of climax quicker. However, all the while, this was building up another wall between me and my husband. I didn't think I was hurting anyone else. This was between me, myself and I. In my humble opinion, I genuinely reasoned in my mind that masturbating and watching porn was better than having a physical affair with another man. But the whole truth of the matter was that I was still committing adultery—against my own body.

In the Word, 1 Corinthians 6:15-20 (MSG) says, *There's more to sex than mere skin on skin. Sex is as much spiritual mystery as physical fact. As written in Scripture, "The two become one." Since we want to become spiritually one with the Master, we must not pursue the kind of sex that avoids commitment and intimacy, leaving us more lonely than ever— the kind of sex that can never "become one." There is a sense in which sexual sins are different from all others. In sexual sin we violate the sacredness of our own bodies, these bodies that were made for God-given and God-modeled love, for "becoming one" with another. Or didn't you realize that your body is a sacred place, the place of the Holy Spirit? Don't you see that you can't live however you please, squandering what God paid such a high price for? The physical part of you is not some piece of property belonging to the spiritual part of you. God owns the whole works. So let people see God in and through your body.*

Eventually, I attended a benefit fundraiser for human trafficking, where victims shared their stories of living in hotel rooms and basements of homes for months. What I learned at that event was truly eye-opening. I didn't know that most of the women in porn are either underage or drugged and forced to perform for the camera. Many of the women who shared their testimonies spent weeks, if not months, in hotel rooms, waiting for the next man to come in and have sex with her as he wished while she was tied up. In essence, when I watched porn, not only was I committing adultery—but I was also silently supporting human trafficking. That was it for me. It took me a while to realize that the women or girls in those films are someone's daughters. Those women and girls are someone's sisters. In order for me to be free, and absolutely free indeed, the Lord asked me some pretty bold questions.

"Would you masturbate in front of your husband or children?"

Hell no!

"Would you stand in the middle of someone else's bedroom and watch another couple have sex?"

God, no!

"If you wouldn't do it in front of your husband or children, and if you wouldn't watch someone else have sex, then don't watch porn or masturbate. It's that simple."

See, if we listen for God's voice, we hear Him crystal clear. We may not like what He says or how He says it. But we do hear Him. It's up to us to choose whether we will be slaves to sin or sold out for God and surrender all to Him! We also have to know that when God asks us a question, He already knows the answer. He's simply asking to make sure that we know the answer. We may not like the answer because we want to please our flesh and please God. Revelation 3:15-17 reminds us that God wants us to either be hot or cold. We can be sold out for God or committed to the things of this world. We can please our flesh, giving into its every desire, or we can please God. I'm not here to perpetrate as if it's always easy to follow God's commandments. But He never promised easy. He promised to never leave us nor forsake us. He promised to make a way of escape out of every trap, snare or affliction the enemy sends our way. He promised to supply our every need (not our wants) according to His riches in glory.

But He never, ever promised *easy*.

If it separates you from God, it's sin. If He told you personally not to do something, and you do it anyway, it's disobedience, which is sin. If it brings you shame and embarrassment, it's sin. If you have to do it in the dark, it's sin. If you have to hide under the covers to do it, it's sin. I was in the church, singing in the choir and praise team, serving in youth ministry—operating in full sin. I was in the church building, but the church wasn't in me. I knew how to do "religion," but I knew nothing about establishing a relationship with Christ. I knew I needed to read the Word, but I didn't know how to rightly divide and interpret the Word.

The five keys we will discuss in detail in the following chapters aren't for every woman who masturbates or watches pornography. They are only for the spiritually mature, not religious, woman who wants to live a life of freedom, healing and wholeness—whether they are single or married. Some women see absolutely nothing wrong with porn or masturbation, especially if they only do it in moderation. This book is less about convincing a woman what's wrong and what's right, and more about helping those women who are *addicted* to porn and masturbation get free once and for all. Though practical in nature, my prayer is that you would take hold of the five keys, implement them into your daily walk with Christ, and become stronger physically, spiritually, mentally and emotionally. It's time to be free and free indeed.

Read at your own risk. When you *know* better, God will require you to *do* better.

KEY 1
ACCOUNTABILITY

For many people, the word "accountability" is a curse word. The average person doesn't like to be told what they can or cannot do. Many people have problems submitting to authority for various reasons, including fear, previous hurt or abuse of power by people they've known and trusted over the years. Nonetheless, we were never meant to do life alone. It was never God's original intent for us to do anything alone. Genesis 2:18 (MSG) says, God said, *"It's not good for the Man to be alone; I'll make him a helper, a companion."* Unfortunately, so many people believe this Scripture only applies to marriage. So, people who aren't married assume they don't have to be accountable to anyone, but God.

Your circle is like an elevator. Either it's taking you up, or it's taking you down.

However, Ecclesiastes 4:9 (NLT) says, *Two people are better off than one, for they can help each other succeed.* That Scripture doesn't say two spouses. It doesn't say husband and wife. It says "two people" are better off than one—which I interpret as *any* two people. Everyone has periods of weakness. Everyone is going to need someone to lift them up, pray for them, carry them through the dark seasons, and walk with them through the tough times of life. Unfortunately for us, but fortunately for the enemy, he uses isolation to attack the sheep one by one.

The enemy knows that, as long as we are surrounded by a community of believers, as long as we can connect with at least one individual of faith, his plan is null and void. He can't win. But the moment he gets one of the sheep backed into a corner, and they choose to unplug from the lifelines, accountability partners, friends and family, the enemy has the upper hand. And let's be clear. When I speak of accountability partners, I'm not speaking of "Yes!" men and women. If your circle always agrees with everything you do and say, you need a new circle. Your circle is like an elevator. Either it's taking you up, or it's taking you down. Otherwise, you're just on the elevator, standing still—which serves absolutely no purpose.

When it comes to breaking free from addiction to porn and masturbation, accountability can look different for everyone. It depends on your level of addiction. You may not be aroused by male strippers or men who flirt with you. But you may not be able to watch Rated R or X movies. You may not be able to go into lingerie shops or sex toy stores. You also may not be able to be alone at home for hours at a time, unattended.

I know this may seem extreme. It may seem like someone is babysitting you. It may seem like that's giving people a whole lot of access to your business. But if you truly want to be free, and free indeed, it's going to take all of this and more.

Accountability could look like you granting access and login information to someone to check your Internet browsing history, your social media history and your TV channel surfing history. Accountability could also look like downloading the Covenant Eyes app and allowing your accountability partner to have access to your cell phone history at all times. Covenant Eyes is designed to help people break free from pornography and stay free. According to Covenant Eyes, 87% of Christian women have watched porn. That's more than half the church, and we know that the majority of the church at-large is made up of women. Out of those 87% of women, only 17% consider themselves to be *addicted* to porn. I'm sure if we asked alcoholics if they considered themselves to be addicted to alcohol, the numbers would be as low, if not more. Most times, the response from any addict who is challenged is, "I can stop whenever I want."

Until you can't.

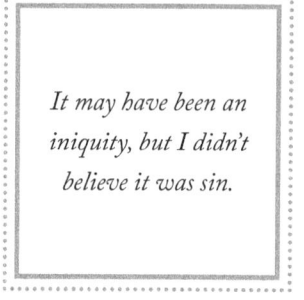

It may have been an iniquity, but I didn't believe it was sin.

Addictions don't play fair. We're in control of a thing until we're not. When you start making excuses for why you need to do something that you know is unhealthy, you're borderline addicted or already too far in to even notice. For years, I convinced myself that watching porn wasn't an outright sin. It may have been an iniquity, but I didn't believe it was sin. Then, after marriage, I convinced myself that I needed porn and masturbation as a tutorial and teaching tool. I wanted to know *what* to do to please my husband. I wanted to know *how* to do what I needed to do to please my husband. Instead, my teaching tool became my nemesis.

When I was really ready to break free, and stay free, I gave certain people in my life permission to ask me at any time, "When was the last time you watched porn? When was the last time you masturbated? When was the last time you even thought about masturbating or watching porn?" Because of our agreement, when they asked, I had to answer with the whole truth. It took me a while to learn that, even if I chose to lie to them, it was only hurting me. I was only lying to *myself.*

Accountability also came in the form of a small community group for me. Others were invested in my freedom and journey to stay free. While I may have been accountable to one or two people daily, I was accountable to my small group community weekly and monthly. In my community group, we didn't just take prayer requests. We asked follow-up questions and for updates on the prayer requests as the group progressed. So, every so often, I had to give an account of where I was in front of the group. If I fell short or gave in to temptation at any point, I wasn't just letting myself down. I was letting a host of people who were praying and interceding for me down.

Matthew 18:20 (MSG) says, "*Take this most seriously: A yes on earth is yes in heaven; a no on earth is no in heaven. What you say to one another is eternal. I mean this. When two of you get together on anything at all on earth and make a prayer of it, my Father in heaven goes into action. And when two or three of you are together because of me, you can be sure that I'll be there.*" There is great power in agreement. That means when two or three people are in agreement about one person breaking free from porn and masturbation addiction, all of Heaven is backing them. So many people only believe that this verse only applies to marriage. But we all have the power to pray the prayers of agreement and believe God has heard us, and He is already working on our behalf.

I also had to be real with myself, and with others, and call someone when I needed help. There were times when the thoughts and the urges to masturbate or watch porn were stronger than others. I had to have a lifeline or two. Sometimes, I needed five lifelines. But I had to be brutally open and honest, and check in with myself to know where I was spiritually, emotionally and physically. When I didn't feel like I could pray it away, fast the thoughts away, or worship the urges away, I knew I needed to call in backup. Now, let's be clear. These weren't people who shamed me or made me feel guilty. They didn't holler or scream at me. They didn't judge me when I called them and said I was having these thoughts and urges. They listened. They prayed. They took me out to lunch or for coffee. They loved me through it. They let me talk and vent. They walked me through the journey of my day or my week to see how I even got back to that place. But they didn't leave me stuck in the hole with my own thoughts and lustful desires. For that, I'm truly grateful.

Ecclesiastes 4:9-12 (NIV) says, *Two are better than one, because they have a good return for their labor: If either of them falls down, one can help the other up. But pity anyone who falls and has no one to help them up. Also, if two lie down together, they will keep warm. But how can one keep warm alone? Though one may be overpowered, two can defend themselves. A cord of three strands is not quickly broken.*

The part of this Scripture that stood out to me is that *if either of them falls down, one can help the other up. But pity anyone who falls and has no one to help them up.* I don't even think it's a matter of if either of them falls down. It should be when either of them falls down. We will all fall down. *But pity* (the feeling of sorrow and compassion caused by the suffering and misfortunes of others) *anyone who falls and has no one to help them up.*

The journey to healing and deliverance from addiction to porn and masturbation is not a journey one can take alone. I would even go so far as to say that you *can* go at it all on your own. You can pray all the prayers and read books. You can fast and ask God to help you break through and break free. But I would venture to say that you can only go so far alone. You may even feel like you're free and that you have the victory over addiction. But it's no different than addiction to crack, alcohol or meth. No one knows what you do behind closed doors but you and God. Real, authentic freedom—and staying free—requires accountability. If you think the enemy is going to let you break free and stay free, and never come knocking at your doorstep with the same lustful desires, you are sadly mistaken. He has one job.

John 10:10 (NIV) says, *The thief comes only to steal and kill and destroy; I have come that they may have life, and have it to the full.* The enemy is on his job 24/7. We need to be intentional about ours. He doesn't have any new tricks. He uses the same things, the same hooks, to draw us back into sin and old lifestyles. You're going to need a lifeline. You're going to need a support group or small group. You're going to need someone you can call when the thoughts, the urges, and the desires come. One thing I can guarantee: They *will* come. It's how you respond, or don't respond, that will determine if you get free and stay free.

UNDERCOVER
Reflections

1. What, if anything, do you fear about true accountability?

_____

_____

_____

_____

_____

_____

2. What three people in your life can best hold you accountable as you walk through this freedom journey and why?

_____

_____

_____

_____

_____

_____

3. What code word or phrase can you say to your accountability partner when you're struggling and need help?

_____

_____

_____

_____

_____

_____

4. As you journey to complete healing and wholeness, who do you need to disconnect from in your circle?

_____

_____

_____

_____

_____

_____

5. Behind closed doors, what is your greatest struggle as it relates to porn/masturbation?

_____

_____

_____

_____

_____

_____

KEY 2
GUARDING YOUR GATES

The year was 1999. An all-male R&B group called Silk released an album called *Tonight*. Now, just in case you weren't even born yet in the 90s, let me let you in on some of the song titles on the album. *Let's Make Love* and *Meeting in My Bedroom* just so happened to be my personal favorites. However, other titles of the songs included *Sexcellent*, *Turn-U-Out* and *Love You Down*. Now, in 1999, I wasn't married. I wasn't even dating anyone exclusively. I was in my third year of college, living my best life in Columbia, Missouri (go, Tigers!). In full transparency, in my freshman year of college, I'd slept with so many men that I couldn't even remember all of their names. I was the center of attention in the club, and I made sure I was both seen and heard. Sheltered by my mother until she dropped me off in COMO, as we affectionately called it, I was wildin' out. I was looking for something, someone. But I don't even know if I knew at the time what or who exactly I was looking for, but I was having fun on the hunt to find it!

So, I often listened to this Silk album as I got dressed for the club in my dorm room. I didn't realize it at the time, but that was the quickest way to get me in a sexy mood to wear the sexy clothes to the club, which often led to a night of sex. Music was my boost of courage. Even if I didn't necessarily feel like going to the club that night, playing one of these songs on the *Tonight* album shifted my energy real quick. I think the song *Meeting in My Bedroom* is pretty self-explanatory, but I'll unpack it anyhow. It chronicles one man's invitation to a woman to come into his bedroom and everything he will do when she gets there. In addition to that, he urges her not to be late. He tells her not to make him wait. Even though I am a woman, I often sang the song like I was the lead singer in the group. It was the thrill, the excitement, the mystery even of what the "meeting in my bedroom" would consist of. But, let's be clear. *My* room was really *our* room because I had a college roommate whom I often put out of the room at night. To this day, Wendy probably hates me.

There was also an artist named Joe, who dropped a song called *All the Things (Your Man Won't Do)*. I won't even unpack Tevin Campbell's *Can We Talk* and Mint Condition's *What Kind of Man Would I Be*. I don't have enough pages in this book to do so. But, if you were growing up in the 90s like I was, these songs just took you back down memory lane. You probably pictured that guy you were crushing on who didn't even notice you. Maybe these songs reminded you of your first official heartbreak, like the Babyface album, *The Day*, does for me. Maybe, when you listen to these songs on Apple Music today, it takes you back to the bedroom boom you had during those years of your life. Maybe you smile; maybe you cry. Either way, know that the mind and the body have kept score. It seems like those thoughts and vivid images may be tucked away

> *If you're going to heal from addiction to porn and masturbation, you've got to guard your ear gates and your eye gates.*

in a locked vault—until you hear that song again. Now, it may be thirty years later, but your whole body starts gyrating, and you start giggling. You don't even know why! You see that guy, that night, that one moment in time that you'd tucked away as foolish childhood ways. I learned through years of counseling that if we have triggers from trauma, we have triggers from those times of joy, laughter, hope, smiles, and yes, even sex and intimacy.

This chapter is less about going down memory lane and more about the *effects* of going down memory lane—or even going too far into the future through your imaginative ways. If you're going to heal from addiction to porn and masturbation, you've got to guard your ear gates and your eye gates. It's important that you watch what you're watching. It's important that you truly listen to what you're listening to. One of my mentors used to say, "Garbage in, garbage out." Now, for years I didn't know what that meant. I thought she was talking about the type of food we eat. I thought she was encouraging me to eat healthier. Matthew 6:22-24 (NLT) says, *"Your eye is like a lamp that provides light for your body. When your eye is healthy, your whole body is filled with light. But when your eye is unhealthy, your whole body is filled with darkness. And if the light you think you have is actually darkness, how deep that darkness is!"*

The Word of God tells us that our eyes are a lamp for the body. That means it lights up the body. When our eyes are healthy, that means the whole body will be healthy. In this sense, the word "healthy" doesn't mean that we're not legally blind or we have natural eyesight problems. It means that what we watch is healthy for us and the body. We have to ask ourselves, "Is what I'm watching edifying me or the body of Christ, or is it drawing me further away from Christ and the body?" As a matter of fact, in those times when I'm not sure, I ask two or three people who have godly wisdom and can steer me in the way that is eternal. Some people will argue that it's not that big of a deal to watch sex scenes in movies or on TV shows. Every man or woman has his or her own convictions. But, for me, even a kiss on TV or the big screen can send me into a horny hole.

I loved the hit show *Empire* that came on Fox for years. The storyline was great, and the actors were even more incredible. The show started out great. There was mad action and drama, keeping me on the edge of my seat every week to see what happened with Cookie (who was my entrepreneurial hero at the time). Somewhere along the lines, the storyline took a turn, and there was more kissing, sex, and fondling than my eyes and ears could stand. At first, I simply tried to skip past those scenes. But eventually, they were intertwined so much into the storyline that I'd miss too much for the episode to make sense if I fast-forwarded. So, I decided to stop watching the show. *How to Get Away with Murder* and *Scandal* became the same way for me. Those shows, too, started out with great storylines, but ended in sex-scapades of all sorts that took me down a rabbit hole I could barely pull myself out of most times. Primetime television on a Thursday night was suddenly rated X, without the expensive subscriptions.

When I got married in 2003, I realized that I needed to get rid of my porn VHS tapes and DVDs if I was going to be free. But I wasn't prepared for the trap of paid cable channels and pay-per-view options right from the comfort of my own living room. My husband didn't understand it at the time, but I told him to cancel all of the premium channels. While we watched great movies during the day on HBO, Cinemax, and Showtime after 11 p.m., those channels automatically switched to "naughty at night" and "dirty after dark" movies. I fell asleep oftentimes with the TV on a premium channel, only to wake up in the middle of the night to sex scenes loud and clear. So, I had to set up another "gate" for my eyes. I couldn't watch premium channels and, apparently, I couldn't watch primetime television.

In addition, I quickly learned that I couldn't blast Silk, Tevin Campbell, Mint Condition or Brian McKnight unless I was in the presence of my husband for the rest of the evening. Call it nostalgia or awakening the sleeping bear of lust way too soon. But going down R&B memory lane, for me, has to be reserved for date nights, road trips, and weekend getaways with the husband. I can listen to some jazz or R&B without it evoking strong emotions, but I know my limits. You should, too. We all have limits and triggers. It's like a trip wire or stepping on a landmine. I learned the hard way, so you don't have to. Lust is never satisfied. It's stronger than any drug or alcohol addiction, and it's always looking and searching for the next high.

Philippians 4:8 (NKJV) says, *Finally, brethren, whatever things are true, whatever things are noble, whatever things are just, whatever things are pure, whatever things are lovely, whatever things are of good report, if there is any virtue and if there is anything praiseworthy—meditate on these things.*

I had to ask myself: *Is porn noble? Are porn and masturbation pure and lovely? Furthermore, is porn of good report?* I knew I wasn't screaming it from the mountaintops or sharing it with friends and family. So, it couldn't have been pure and lovely. It couldn't have been of good report. I knew it wasn't of good report because there was a strong sense of shame that came along with watching porn and masturbating shortly after every act. Yet, the urges only got stronger. The flesh wouldn't sit still, and it wouldn't calm down on its own. Lust doesn't play fair. So, I knew I had to play a different game.

Guarding my eye gates was almost more pivotal than guarding my ear gates. There's a famous quote that says, "The eyes are the window to the soul." The eyes reflect our emotions, our desires, our hurts, our fears, the years of tears, and our joys. For years, I walked with my head down. I never wanted to look anyone in the eye. I was afraid people would *see* me, the *real* me. I was afraid people would see my broken heart, the scars, the wounds, and the wounded soul that I worked hard to keep hidden behind a mask. If the eyes can tell that much of a story, what we watch, what we see, and what we allow in through those gates is pivotal. It's amazing how the eyes can speak without a person saying a word.

> *Guard your gates like your very life depends on it— because it truly does.*

Whether you know it or not, what you listen to and what you watch is what will influence your life. If the concept of "garbage in, garbage out" is true, then that means if we put good things into our ear gates and eye gates, good things will come out. If we feed ourselves sex, lust, porn and masturbation thoughts, that is the direction in which our lives will follow. You may have heard people say, "Your life will follow the road of your strongest thought." So, whatever you think of the most is what will rule and reign. Whatever you focus on the most is what will grow.

Guard your gates like your very life depends on it—because it truly does.

UNDERCOVER
Reflections

1. What top three TV shows or movies will you stop watching to ensure success on your journey to freedom?

_____

_____

_____

_____

_____

_____

2. What top three albums or artists do you need to delete from your music library to protect your ear gates?

_____

_____

_____

_____

_____

_____

3. What three people in your life can offer you godly wisdom and steer you in the way eternal when you're not sure if you're in alignment with God?

_____

_____

_____

_____

_____

_____

4. What emails or subscriptions do you need to unsubscribe from to guard your gates?

_____

_____

_____

_____

_____

_____

5. If your life follows the road of your strongest thought, in what direction is your life heading?

_____

_____

_____

_____

_____

_____

KEY 3
PRAYER AND FASTING

atthew 17:21 (AMP) says, *But this kind of demon does not go out except by prayer and fasting.* While I've been familiar with this Scripture for years, it wasn't until I decided to truly break free from the stronghold of addiction to porn and masturbation that I implemented it into my life. Ironically, when my husband and I used to fast every Wednesday with our church from midnight to 4 p.m., not only was I strong enough not to eat food, but I was cognizant enough not to watch porn or masturbate during that specific time of fasting. That strength was often short-lived, usually just for that day. If I was truly going to have victory over this addiction, I had to do something different.

Most people pray before they lay down to sleep. Others may pray briefly when they bless their food or right before a big job interview. Some people even spend significant time in prayer for family members, a health concern, or for the nation at-large. However, few take the time to pray and fast for their own healing and deliverance from addiction. They may be saved, and they know where they're going when they pass away. But they are not intentionally praying and fasting to break free from the chains of porn and masturbation. Prayer doesn't happen by osmosis; yet it's one of the most underrated secret weapons of Kingdom citizens.

In the above passage in Matthew, Jesus is responding to the disciples' frustrated inquiry about why they couldn't cast a demon out that Jesus so calmly came onto the scene and handled. Most Christians understand the *importance* of prayer, but they may not understand the *power* of prayer. Even more so, the average Christian doesn't have a problem with prayer. But when challenged to fast, some Christians decline the challenge. Some people don't believe "it takes all that" to get the healing and breakthrough one desires. Others simply don't want to crucify their flesh. They want to eat what they want to eat, listen to what they want to listen to and watch what they want to watch. While we should be able to hear God's voice daily, His voice is often mixed in with the noise of our workday, social media, phone calls, and other distractions that are fighting for our attention. Over time, this makes it harder to hear Him.

In my walk with Christ, I've learned that prayer yields results. Fasting yields results. But the combination of the two working simultaneously yields something altogether different. Whether I'm fasting from food, social media, TV, the phone—or a combination of all of those—I can hear

God more often and more clearly. It's almost as if my ears have been unplugged and I can hear God's voice amplified like a stereo. Likewise, I see things I've never seen before. I notice things I may not have otherwise noticed. I get divine downloads on how to pray, what to pray, how to move forward in business and ministry, and more. More often than not, when I'm fasting and praying, God downloads strategies or words of encouragement for me to give others I'm connected to, not necessarily for myself. I've learned that God is not going to shout and scream to get our attention above all the other things we have fighting for our attention on any given day.

> *But if we're looking for the next strategy or seeking Him for direction on healing and deliverance, we've got to be willing to sit still and listen for instruction.*

First Kings 19:11-13 (NIV) says, *The Lord said, "Go out and stand on the mountain in the presence of the Lord, for the Lord is about to pass by." Then a great and powerful wind tore the mountains apart and shattered the rocks before the Lord, but the Lord was not in the wind. After the wind there was an earthquake, but the Lord was not in the earthquake. After the earthquake came a fire, but the Lord was not in the fire. And after the fire came a gentle whisper. When Elijah heard it, he pulled his cloak over his face and went out and stood at the mouth of the cave. Then a voice said to him, "What are you doing here, Elijah?"*

So many times, we're looking for God in the big boom. We think that the louder a worship service is or the louder a preacher ministers, the more God is speaking. Unfortunately, it's usually the opposite. I have found God to speak more in a worship service where people are kneeling or sitting in silence, with soft music playing, than in the services where there is screaming, yelling and shouting. Yes, we should offer shouts of praise. Yes, we should celebrate all that the King of kings and Lord of lords has done for us. But if we're looking for the next strategy or seeking Him for direction on healing and deliverance, we've got to be willing to sit still and listen for instruction.

Prayer should not be a monologue. God isn't a genie waiting for us to ask for our next wish. He wants to have intimate conversations with us built on our call and his response. Even though He already knows we can't make it without Him, He wants us to tell him. Even though He knows we need Him, He wants to hear it. I'm just crazy enough to believe that when we truly surrender our hearts, our minds and our mouths to the Lord, He will give us the keys, the strategies, and the wisdom to break free from the strongholds that have tortured so many of us for years.

To truly break free from the chains of porn and masturbation will require prayer and fasting. Unfortunately, too many people pray once and fast once, and they don't see the victory. So, they, in turn, argue that prayer and fasting don't work. If addiction to porn and masturbation was a form of cancer, would you take one chemo treatment and one radiation treatment, and quit if neither of those treatments didn't kill the cancer on contact? The average person who has any form of cancer works with their doctor to create a treatment action plan for the months ahead, if not the years ahead. Typically, a cancer patient won't stop in the middle of the treatment plan unless a doctor advises them that the treatment simply isn't working. But when it comes to fasting and prayer, we often quit too soon. In a perfect world, we would pray once and fast once, get victory, and live a life of freedom forever. But because we live in a fallen world, we are always praying. We are always going to be challenged to fast. Prayer and fasting aren't one-time events; they have to become a lifestyle.

When I didn't know what to pray to break free from my addiction to porn and masturbation, God first shifted my perspective. I knew Exodus 20:3 (NIV) says, *"You shall have no other gods before me."* What I didn't know was that I had made porn and masturbation my god, unintentionally. I'll never forget the moment when God spoke these words to me: "Anything or anyone you obey more than me is now your god." I was shaken. I knew I didn't worship golden calves or statues of Buddha. In my ignorance, that was my limited definition of other gods. But in those days when I was on the seesaw of obeying God's Word, versus masturbation or watching porn, porn and masturbation won the battle too many times to count.

I knew that the Bible spoke against idolatry and making idols out of other people and things. Leviticus 26:1 (NIV) says, "*Do not make idols or set up an image or a sacred stone for yourselves, and do not place a carved stone in your land to bow down before it. I am the Lord your God.*" While I hadn't set up a physical stone or image as an idol, and I hadn't bowed to a

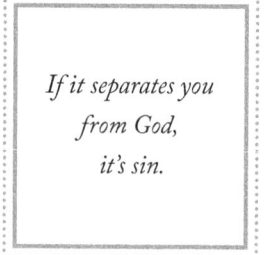

If it separates you from God, it's sin.

physical replica of an idol, at some point, porn and masturbation became my idol. I thought about it more than God or even the Word of God daily. I spent more time masturbating than I did reading the Word of God or in prayer. The struggle and the seesaw eventually became a surrender. I gave myself over to porn and masturbation as a way of life I'd never break free from. It was my "thorn" and my "cross" that I had to carry, which is why God first had to change my mindset. Otherwise, for years, I didn't see the sin in it.

Spoiler alert: If it separates you from God, it's sin.

Once my mindset shifted to transforming my will to do life God's way, God said, "When you don't know what to pray, pray my Word or pray in tongues." Philippians 4:8 says, *Finally, brethren, whatsoever things are true, whatsoever things are honest, whatsoever things are just, whatsoever things are pure, whatsoever things are lovely, whatsoever things are of good report; if there be any virtue, and if there be any praise, think on these things.* So, I prayed, "God, help me to think on those things that are pure, those things that are honest, those things that are pure, lovely and just." Many times, I prayed, "No weapon (thought, idea, imagination, person, or spirit) formed against me shall prosper and greater is He that is in me than he that is in the world." I asked God to help me to keep my mind stayed on Him and on things above. I asked Him to turn my heart back to my first love. My one desire was to live a life that was pleasing before God. Now, don't get it twisted. That doesn't mean the enemy still didn't send the same darts (thoughts) my way. After all, he had won the battle so many years prior. Why would this time be any different? He didn't have to create anything new. He *can't* create anything new. He is not the Creator. For years, I'd given him access, a key to the front door of my heart and mind, to come in and introduce thoughts and ideations that didn't align with God and His Word. I knew I couldn't fully evict him without the help and the strength of God.

When most people hear the word fasting, they translate it as "starving and not eating." Not eating food is a part of fasting, but it doesn't end there. I've found that if I'm attempting to fast from food, but I'm still watching secular shows on TV or scrolling social media for hours on end, I may as well eat. I'm not hearing God clearly. I'm not focused on the Word, and I'm not getting any direction or strategy for what's next. Referring back to our first couple of keys, I have to operate in a lifestyle of fasting from certain things and even people. For example, I no longer watch the news. I unsubscribed from all news apps, as well. I found that watching the news kept me glued to the TV in anxiety and fear, as if I could control what happens in the world at-large. I can't listen to certain songs or certain types of music that have extensive profanity or sexual connotations. It takes me right back to my college days and/or it plants seeds for me to act on those fleshly urges. Usually, I do not listen to R&B or even Neo Soul unless it's date night with my husband or we're on vacation together without the kids. Yes, music, for me, is that powerful that it almost instantaneously shifts my mood and mindset.

Another form of fasting we often overlook is fasting from negative people and negative conversations. Gossip and shady conversations can be just as detrimental to the mind and heart as addiction to drugs or alcohol. If the power of death and life truly lies in the power of the tongue, that means we get to choose. We have to choose to shut down gossip. We have to choose not to answer the phone calls or text messages that come with stress, strife, discord and bad-mouthing others. If you're not sure if a conversation is negative or considered gossip, ask yourself, "How does this advance the Kingdom of God or glorify God?" If it doesn't, cut the conversation short. We can gracefully cut conversations short by either ending the phone call or changing the subject. If you don't see any easy way to transition, say to the person on the other end, "Well, let's pray for the person/situation right now!" That turns the gossip into a prayer moment. We always have a choice. We get to decide what comes out of our mouths or what we allow ourselves to take in from someone or somewhere else. If we want to experience life, we must speak life—not simply repeat what we see or what others have said. In order to truly be the called-out ones, the set-apart ones, we must say something different so we can see something different. You will know if you need to fast from a person or certain conversations—for a season or for a lifetime.

I could give you specific formulas and timelines of how to fast and what to fast from. But ultimately, you want to be led by God. He knows what's best for you. Each person is different. What works for me may not work for you to break free from porn and masturbation addiction. You may have to set up more accountability, or you may have to avoid beaches. It all depends on what you need to truly break free from the addiction. For example, I have to leave the room or change the channel during sex scenes on TV or in a movie. It's too much for me, but that doesn't mean it may be too much for you. The Holy Spirit will make it plain what you *can* and *cannot* do. He will make it plain what you *can* and *cannot* watch or listen to. It may not be a sin to others. But if God tells you not to do it—and you indulge in it anyway—it's sin for you.

UNDERCOVER
Reflections

1. How often do you fast outside of corporate prayer and fasting with a ministry?

_____

_____

_____

_____

_____

_____

2. What do you need to fast from besides food?

_____

_____

_____

_____

_____

_____

3. How will you change your conversations after today?

_____

_____

_____

_____

_____

_____

4. What idols or other gods have you unintentionally set up in your heart that need to be torn down?

_____

_____

_____

_____

_____

_____

5. What three verses of Scripture can you meditate on as you fast and pray on your journey to freedom?

_____

_____

_____

_____

_____

_____

KEY 4
HEALTHY REPLACEMENTS

When it comes to the world of food, nutritionists worldwide have laundry lists of healthy alternatives to almost every piece of food one loves to consume in order for a person to develop a healthy diet. Many people replace bagels with English muffins. One might replace regular coffee creamer with almond milk. While some people replace mayo with hummus, others replace rice with riced cauliflower. On Taco Tuesday, some people replace sour cream with Greek yogurt. Instead of snacking on candy and chips, someone may opt for a trail mix where they can fulfill both the sweet and the salty cravings all in one. It sounds so simple; yet I know firsthand that just because I *know* there is a healthy alternative doesn't mean I always *choose* the healthy alternative.

> *There is no one-size-fits-all formula for healing and breaking free from old, unhealthy habits.*

That's the dangerous part. We still have a choice in the matter. We have *free will*.

Older studies show that it takes twenty-one days to make something a habit. Then, over time, researchers moved the mark to sixty to ninety days. I'm under the impression now that it may look different for everyone. Everyone's measure of willpower is different. I've learned that what takes one person ninety days to conquer may take nine years for another person to master. There is no one-size-fits-all formula for healing and breaking free from old, unhealthy habits. Addiction to porn and masturbation is no different. It will take not only healthy replacements to get free, but also to stay *free* and free indeed.

When it comes to addiction to porn and masturbation, healthy replacements may look different for you than it does for others. My greatest healthy replacement to date has been focus and productivity. When I'm not publishing someone's next bestseller, coaching a writing client or ghostwriting, I'm working on my personal projects. I always have another book to write. I always have another stage production or script to work on. I'm always gearing up for the next transformational event, even if it's six months away. Many times, I verbally have to tell myself, "Girl! We don't have time to waste! Get busy!" For many, the word "busy" doesn't equate to focus and productivity. But when I've got my head down writing my next bestseller, it's hard to step away just to watch porn or to masturbate.

Instead of movies or TV shows that have a lot of sex scenes, profanity or vulgarity, I'm watching inspirational YouTube videos, repeat episodes of Sunday sermons online, or motivational vlogs. As I matured in age and in my walk with Christ, I realized that I couldn't listen to local radio. I don't listen to the national morning shows or even the local talk shows. There is too much vying for my attention that I can't control. I can't control what the radio stations discuss on air, but I can control what I listen to in the car. So, if I'm not listening to worship music or jazz, I'm probably listening to a podcast I've been waiting to dig into.

Even though I read books, I hardly ever read eBooks on my phone or iPad. Again, there are too many paid ads, notifications and alerts vying for my attention when I'm on an electronic device. I've tried reading eBooks on my phone, as well as on my iPad. Both are equally distracting for me. If anything, I may purchase a basic Kindle eReader just to read eBooks. Even though the Kindle eReader has Wi-Fi, it doesn't have social media apps. The purpose of the Wi-Fi is solely to be able to download eBooks from Amazon. However, there's something unique about turning the pages of a physical book. Nothing can compare to highlighting, underlining and marking up the physical pages of a book. When I flip through a physical book for a second or third time, sometimes I just read the highlights. I only take the time to review those highlighted nuggets I captured while

> *As you progress in your healing journey, you're going to have friends and family members who don't understand.*

I was reading the book the first time. So, I get to study the information without the numerous distractions that come with a phone or any other electronic device.

Speaking of healthy replacements, on your journey of healing from addiction to porn and masturbation, you're going to have to replace some *people*. That may mean family. It may mean getting a new set of friends. For me, it meant getting a new counselor, even. My first professional counselor helped me significantly get to the root of many problems. However, she was not a Christian counselor, nor did she counsel based on Christian principles. So, when I told her I wanted to work toward being free from porn and masturbation, she didn't understand.

"What's the problem?" she asked. "Many men and women do it. It's completely natural."

It was that day, in that session, that I realized she had taken me as far as she could take me on my healing journey. It was clear that our belief systems were not aligned. What was sin and a stronghold to me wasn't a worry of hers at all. She saw no fault in it. So, as much as I loved her as a therapist, I knew I had to shift.

As you progress in your healing journey, you're going to have friends and family members who don't understand.

They don't see anything wrong with watching porn and masturbating. As a matter of fact, many friends and family members may even encourage it! Men say things like, "Boys will be boys," when validating why boys or men masturbate. Women are encouraged at bachelorette parties to drink out of penis-sized straws, eat penis-sized gummies, engage with strippers and more—all in the name of fun. It's all fun and games until you're married, and you realize you've already made a replacement for your spouse before you've even said, "I do!" It's all innocent play until your first thought, when you're alone, is to masturbate or turn on porn. You have to surround yourself with like-minded individuals who are going in the same direction. Be intentional about surrounding yourself with individuals who have the mind of Christ.

This may be one of the hardest parts of your healing journey. It can be challenging to turn away from people who you know and love. It can be hard to cut off communication with high school or college friends simply because your life is going in a different direction and your belief systems no longer align. I don't claim to have mastered the art of leaving people and letting them go. I am yet a work in progress. But I've also found that when I try to hang on to people long after I know I should have stepped away, either they begin to pull me in the other direction, or we experience great conflict that causes us to cease communication anyway. I also learned that if I stop calling and wait to see how long it takes certain people to call, I get a wake-up call. They never call. That tells me that the relationship was solely based on my reaching out to them. It was one-sided. But you never know that until you simply stop calling and stop reaching out, and you see firsthand how long it takes for them to reach out to you. It's hurtful, but it's unapologetically eye-opening. Once your eyes have been opened to the truth, you can no longer ignore it.

Matthew 12:43-45 (NLT) says, *"When an evil spirit leaves a person, it goes into the desert, seeking rest but finding none. Then it says, 'I will return to the person I came from.' So, it returns and finds its former home empty, swept, and in order. Then the spirit finds seven other spirits more evil than itself, and they all enter the person and live there. And so that person is worse off than before. That will be the experience of this evil generation."*

It's not enough to get free. It's not enough to break free from the addiction of porn and masturbation without replacing it with something. The average person isn't living inside a home without furniture. Only homeless people and/or what we would call squatters would occupy abandoned or unoccupied homes. Legally, these people don't pay rent. They don't own homes. They usually don't have heat, running water or lights. But to be free from the weather elements, and to avoid sleeping on the streets (literally), many squatters find a home that may be for sale or a home that may be foreclosed on to live. It's not legal. But because the owner has abandoned the home, or the home has simply been vacant for an extended period of time, squatters will use the opportunity to occupy the space.

When you are truly healed, delivered and set free from porn and masturbation addiction, you must fill your "home" with "furniture." If we are the body, if we are the house, Holy Spirit is the furniture. It's not enough for us to sweep our minds, bodies and souls clean. We have to fill the house with the Word of God. We have to fill the house with Holy Spirit. The Message version of Matthew 12:43-45 says, "*When a defiling evil spirit is expelled from someone, it drifts along through the desert looking for an oasis, some unsuspecting soul it can bedevil. When it doesn't find anyone, it says, 'I'll go back to my old haunt.' On return it finds the person spotlessly clean, but vacant. It then runs out and rounds up seven other spirits more evil than itself and they all move in, whooping it up. That person ends up far worse off than if he'd never gotten cleaned up in the first place. "That's what this generation is like: You may think you have cleaned out the junk from your lives and gotten ready for God, but you weren't hospitable to my kingdom message, and now all the devils are moving back in.*"

You're not just in a fight to *get* free. You're in a fight to *stay* free. Let me explain it this way. I've tried many weight loss programs. Most of them helped me to do just that: lose weight. Many of them even allowed me to lose weight *quickly*. However, every time I lost weight, I went right back to eating the same way I did before I started the program. The replacements were temporary (and, oftentimes, expensive), so I couldn't maintain the weight loss long-term. More times than not, I actually gained *more* weight than I'd lost on the program. Sometimes it took six months. Other times, it took a year. But every time, the weight came back *greater*.

That's just one tangible example of Matthew 12:43-45. The bottom line is if you break free from addiction to porn and masturbation. Still, if you don't have healthy replacements, you will surely end up worse off than you were before you got cleaned up in the first place.

UNDERCOVER Reflections

1. What unhealthy movies or TV shows will you replace, and what will you watch instead?

_____

_____

_____

_____

_____

_____

2. What radio stations or shows will you replace, and what will you listen to instead?

_____

_____

_____

_____

_____

_____

3. Who do you need to disengage with in order to ensure success on your journey to freedom?

_____

_____

_____

_____

_____

_____

4. Besides the Word of God, what three things can you immediately replace with the time you would usually spend watching porn or masturbating?

_____

_____

_____

_____

_____

_____

5. What apps on your phone can you delete and/or replace to help you stay free on the journey?

_____

_____

_____

_____

_____

_____

KEY 5
TRANSFORM YOUR MIND

omans 12:22 (NIV) says, *Do not conform to the pattern of this world, but be transformed by the renewing of your mind. Then you will be able to test and approve what God's will is—his good, pleasing and perfect will.* The New Living Translation says, *Don't copy the behavior and customs of this world, but let God transform you into a new person by changing the way you think. Then you will learn to know God's will for you, which is good and pleasing and perfect.*

I tried many times before the last time to break free from my addiction to porn and masturbation. I was always exhausted afterward. After the act, I always had to take a long nap, which caused me to waste even more hours in a day. When the thoughts entered my mind, it was always a tug of war. *Do I forsake all of God's promises for a moment of pleasure? How far away will this one moment in time push me back from every prophecy that was spoken over my life? Since God is a forgiving God, I can just repent afterward. He will forgive me if I just do it this one time ... one more time. I'm not hurting anyone else. It's not really sin if no one else is involved.*

More times than not, the latter thoughts won more than the former. I was fully persuaded in my own mind that what I was doing wasn't hurting anyone else. And, for a season, I didn't even believe I was hurting myself. But it

> *Even with every external resource that was stripped away from my immediate reach, my thoughts and my imagination were enough to keep me in the never-ending cycle of self-satisfying—while at the same time, never being satisfied at all.*

was always the feeling and the fatigue after the moment was over that left me questioning why I kept finding myself in a pattern of satisfying self, yet feeling horrible after it was all over. I'd tried to stop masturbating and watching porn on my own for too many years to count. Even when I got rid of the DVDs, CDs and VHS tapes, I was left with my own imagination. I was still the common denominator. Even with every external resource that was stripped away from my immediate reach, my thoughts and my imagination were enough to keep me in the never-ending cycle of self-satisfying—while at the same time, never being satisfied at all. That's when I realized that we are, more times than not, our own worst enemy.

Proverbs 23:7 (NASB) says, *For as he thinks within himself, so he is.* The Good News Translation says, "*Come on and have some more," he says, but he doesn't mean it. What he thinks is what he really is.* Since I was fully persuaded in my mind that what I was doing was harmless, and I wasn't certain if it was sin or not, I was stuck. I needed someone or something to interrupt the pattern. I was looking for someone or something to get me out of the never-ending cycle. I was tired of going in circles, but I was intrigued by the pleasure. I loved Jesus, but I was easily lured by lust. The Pandora's Box of lust had been opened to me at the age of seven, and I didn't have the lock or the key to contain the beast. Over the years, I'd heard many pastors preach and teach against fornication, "shacking up" and even adultery. But I can count on one hand how many times I heard a pastor teach about the effects of pornography and masturbation. I even heard some pastors say that it was okay as long as you and your spouse engaged in porn and masturbation together. For many churches and church leaders, unfortunately, it's been a grey area.

In the Word, 1 Peter 1:16 (MSG) says, *God said, "I am holy; you be holy."* So, I had to ask myself, "Is masturbation and watching porn holy?" The fact that I had to do it in the dark or under the covers let me know that it was not holy, by far. If we're using Jesus as the role model, I had to ask myself, "Did Jesus ever engage in porn or masturbation?" Nope. Nada. Aside from the Sunday morning sermons, whether they addressed the topic or not, I had to think about *myself* for *myself*. I had to go to God for myself for clarity. Proverbs 23:7 (AMP) says, *For as he thinks in his heart, so is he [in behavior—one who manipulates].* Whatever you believe in your heart and soul (your mind, will, and emotions) will determine your actions. Romans 14:5 (CEV) says, *Some of the Lord's followers think one day is more important than another. Others think all days are the same. But each of you should make up your own mind.* To you, I say, make up your own mind.

So many times, we as believers are looking for our pastors and church leaders to tell us what to do. After all, many times, it's easier to seek wisdom from man than it is for us to take the time to pray, fast and seek God for ourselves. While I'm grateful for pastors and spiritual leaders/mentors, every person should have a personal, intimate relationship with the Father for themselves. Just like a daughter who lives in the house with her father can go ask him questions, likewise, as daughters of the King, we have direct access to ask our Father questions. We can't be afraid of the answers simply because they may make us uncomfortable. As a matter of fact, more times than not, God's perfect will for our lives will require us to get out of our comfort zone.

It's easy to judge the woman who has multiple children out of wedlock with multiple fathers. But, from the perspective of the Kingdom of God, addiction to pornography is no different. It can be easy to crucify a woman who is addicted to cocaine and meth. But, from the perspective of the Kingdom, addiction to masturbation is no different. I had to have a mindset shift. Romans 14:5 (KJV) says, *Let every man be fully persuaded in his* [or her] *own mind.* For years, I was fully persuaded that there was absolutely nothing wrong with watching porn and masturbation. As a matter of fact, I was using it as a gatekeeper so I wouldn't fall into the "big" sins of fornication or adultery. Newsflash: There are no *big* or *little* sins in the Kingdom of God. Sin is sin. God levels the playing field for us all. I knew that if I was going to be truly free, and free indeed from the addiction, I had to be fully persuaded in my mind why I should *not* engage in porn and masturbation.

The first shift in my mindset took place when my pastor friend asked me blatantly, "Are you a prostitute?" My first thought process was to deny it. But since a prostitute is a person who engages in sexual activity for payment, I had to think twice. Even though I wasn't receiving any cash, fancy dinners or expensive handbags after I masturbated, I was singlehandedly responsible for sexually pleasing a body that did not belong to me. As a single, young adult, my body belonged to the Lord. However, I didn't know it at the time. It was 1 Corinthians 6:19 (CEV) that opened my eyes to this fact: *You surely know that your body is a temple where the Holy Spirit lives. The Spirit is in you and is a gift from God. You are no longer your own.* Even though I didn't know much about

Holy Spirit when I got this revelation, I knew that Holy Spirit didn't dwell in houses filled with lust and sexual activities.

Things became even more confusing once I got married, especially when I'd heard numerous preachers, teachers and prophets use Hebrews 13:4 to validate couples engaging in porn and masturbation together. This Scripture in The Message version says, *Honor marriage, and guard the sacredness of sexual intimacy between wife and husband. God draws a firm line against casual and illicit sex.* The only problem with that was the fact that I *never* wanted to engage in it with my husband in the room. I was too shameful and afraid of what he would think. Honestly, I told myself that I *needed* the porn and masturbation to knock the edge off before my husband came home from work. But that plan backfired. That temporary fix, unfortunately, became a permanent replacement for my husband. Many nights, I didn't even pursue sexual intimacy with him because I'd already pleased myself multiple times in one day. He didn't stand a fighting chance. I'd also convinced myself that I needed to use porn as a "training guide" on how to best please my husband. Isn't it amazing how we ask Holy Spirit for help in *some* areas, but not for help in *all* areas of our lives? In hindsight, that was simply one more excuse for me to engage in what I knew didn't feel right.

The Word in 1 Corinthians 7:4 (NLV) says, *The wife is not the boss of her own body. It belongs to the husband. And in the same way, the husband is not the boss of his own body. It belongs to the wife.* That means, even in marriage, I was having sex with a body that belonged to someone else—no matter how convinced I was that my body was my own. I had to look at it this way: It was as if I was having an affair with another man's wife. When you put it into words blatantly like that, it throws up a glaring red flag that I couldn't deny.

More than anything, I wanted to be pleasing to God. I wanted to be pleasing to my husband. I wanted to be counted as righteous and at least *attempt* to live holy. I don't believe God punishes those who sin, then repents and turns away from the sin. It's when we keep on sinning, and we constantly give into the same temptation, that God is judging us. Hebrews 10:26-27 (NIV) says, *If we deliberately keep on sinning after we have received the knowledge of the truth, no sacrifice for sins is left, but only a fearful expectation of judgment and of raging fire that will consume the enemies of God.* So many times, I'd been conflicted and confronted with the truth of what addiction to porn and masturbation was—yet, I chose to ignore the truth. Many people think they want to know the truth until that truth makes them uncomfortable and causes them to change their lifestyle. Everyone wants to hear the truth until it challenges them to face their habits and why they've been holding on to them for so long. Christians love to pray against strongholds. But what do you do when the stronghold you're praying against is *you*? It's your free will. It's your mindset regarding sin. It's your heart that's not totally submitted to God. That's the stronghold.

The enemy isn't that cunning. He can't create anything new. He uses the same tactics and darts to trap God's people. Three main areas he targets are the lust of the eyes, the lust of the flesh, and the pride of life. He really doesn't have to try anything new. Everything the enemy throws at us will more than likely fall into

> *I had to renew my mind to the fact that the enemy can only make suggestions. He can only plant seeds of doubt…*

one of those three categories—if not all three. I had to renew my mind to the fact that the enemy can only make suggestions. He can only plant seeds of doubt to make me think something different than what God said was true or right. Just because he sows seeds doesn't mean we have to let those seeds take root. Just because the enemy shoots darts at my mind doesn't mean I have to take that thought and meditate on it day and night.

Joyce Meyer wrote a life-changing book, *The Battlefield of the Mind*. Throughout the book, she emphasizes the fact that the enemy fights us in our minds *first*. He's not after our houses and cars. He's not mad when we go to church every Sunday. He's not moved when we simply go through the religious motions, and we never live a life of freedom because our minds haven't been transformed. We can only strategically combat the enemy's darts when we know who we are and whose we are! The Word of God is clear: We transform our minds by meditating on the Word of God day and night. If we choose *not* to read and study the Word on a regular basis, our mind will automatically replay the bad. We will subconsciously rehearse our problems instead of God's promises. We will spend hours in depression instead of devotion. We will see nothing but the valley when God has promised us the victory.

I could have listed ten tips or eight steps to break free from addiction to porn and masturbation. But the whole truth of the matter is that, if you don't transform the way you think about porn and masturbation, every key and tip I give is null and void. It won't stick. You've got to think about what you're thinking about. And, unfortunately, no one can do this type of work for you. Sure, you have accountability partners along the way. But this is still a deep, intimate, personal work that must be completed by you and you alone.

For years, I believed I'd never be free from porn and masturbation. It became a part of my very being—until it wasn't. Either Christ dying on the cross was enough for *all* sins, or it wasn't payment for *any* sins. He didn't leave anything incomplete or half-done. He died once and for all, for all. His blood was enough. But, more than likely, He's not going to supernaturally transform our minds. He's going to do it over time as we dive into His Word. All of the answers you need to break free from porn and masturbation may not be in *this book*.

But it's in *His Book*.

John 8:36 (ERV) says, *So if the Son makes you free, you are really free.*

Be healed. Be whole. Be set free!

Closing prayer

Father God, I thank you that your Word promises that He who the Son sets free is free indeed. Thank you for freeing me from the shackles of lust. Thank you for freeing me from the bondage of addiction to pornography and masturbation. Father God, help me guard my ear gates and my eye gates. Help me focus on things that are pure, lovely, and of good report. Father God, surround me with like-minded individuals who will hold me accountable to your standard of holiness and righteousness. Help me to forsake my plan for your eternal plan for my life. Order my steps to keep me on the straight and narrow pathway you have set before me. I thank you that no weapon formed against me from the enemy or the inner me shall prosper in the name of Jesus. Thank you for allowing me to walk in healing and wholeness, and thank you for giving me the ability to unlock others to do the same. I give you all the praise, honor and glory for the work you have done and every great and perfect thing you will do in the days to come. In Jesus' name! Amen!

ABOUT
TENITA C. JOHNSON

*T*ransforming pain into purpose is a gift that authorpreneur, speaker and book coach, Tenita "Bestseller" Johnson gives to everyone she encounters. She is a warrior of words with a fierce passion for guiding authors to expand their brand by showing them how to earn multiple streams of income from just ONE book. As the author of 23 books, seven of which have been Amazon bestsellers, she is living proof that sharing your story leads to your destiny.

Familiar with rising from numerous fires and coming out unscathed, Tenita has triumphed over suicidal thoughts, depression, low self-esteem, marital storms and blended family woes. She has also endured miscarriages and the still birth of twins the day after she married her husband. Each of these tragedies has added indelible layers to her resilience. With more than 25 years in journalism, writing and editing, she has a knack for creating narratives that are authentic and raw, yet endearingly relatable. She is a vessel with the ability to change lives and impact the world, thus she is a proud "book bully," who relentlessly urges others to, "Write the book and get paid for the pain!"

When Tenita speaks, people listen with their ears as well as their hearts and souls because her transparency transcends pretense. She is a bold beacon of hope who inspires others to seek their highest peak. One of her proudest and defining moments was her appearance on Kirk Franklin's Praise Sirius XM channel.

As the founder and CEO of So It Is Written Publishing, she has helped hundreds of authors birth their books in record time. The company excels as a one stop shop for the complete book process from conception to completion, not just editing. The editorial guru successfully helps people to pen books that will boost their brand, accelerate their paydays and bust open doors of endless opportunities. So It Is Written won The Sunrise Pinnacle Award for Diversity Company of the Year, in 2020, from the Rochester Regional Chamber of Commerce in Rochester, Michigan. For six years, Tenita hosted the Red Ink Conference in Atlanta, Detroit, Charlotte and Chicago. Over 600 attendees received invaluable information from industry leaders on how to write, edit, market and publish their next bestseller.

Beyond her books, her versatility shines in multiple areas, including her role as the executive producer of the hit stage play, *When the Smoke Clears*, which was based on her book,

When the Smoke Clears: A Phoenix Rises. The play ran in 2017 and 2018 to sold-out audiences in downtown Detroit. She also served as the editorial director for *Career Mastered Magazine* and *Hope for Women Magazine*.

Tenita's passion for delivering bestselling books is matched only by her devotion to helping women and men heal from the drama, trauma and baggage of sexual abuse. Her 2021 anthology, *HUSH: Breaking the Cycle of Silence Around Sexual Abuse*, featured eight women who lost their innocence and identity to life-altering trauma. She is a huge advocate and mouthpiece for those who have been sexually abused as she empowers them to release their pain instead of suffering in silence.

Her future plans include producing her short film *What Happens in This House* and completing the script for her feature film *When the Smoke Clears*. As a catalyst for positive change, she is a woman who has learned to live an intentional life of purpose while unapologetically fulfilling her God-driven assignments.

For booking or speaking engagements, email info@soitiswritten.net or visit www.tenitajohnson.com.

ABOUT
SO IT IS WRITTEN

 We help Christian female speakers and coaches write the ONE book that will expand their reach and get them to SIX figures in record time! Period!

As the leading content curators for six-figure authorpreneurs and entrepreneurs, So It Is Written is best known for helping them package and leverage their expertise into a bestselling book, which amplifies their brand, accelerates their paydays and attracts bigger opportunities!

Let us help you brand in excellence as an author and entrepreneur so you can develop multiple streams of income from just ONE book!

Call us at 313-777-8607 today or email info@soitiswritten.net for more details about our services. We look forward to working with you to make your project one of excellence!

www.ingramcontent.com/pod-product-compliance
Lightning Source LLC
Chambersburg PA
CBHW060346130626
46553CB00003B/1109